MORTGAGE FREE

Becoming Mortgage Free Without Sacrificing Your Lifestyle.

K. ELIZABETH

©2016

Table of Contents

Introduction

If you, like me are tired of living a life of undue financial strain, then this book is for you!

I distinctly remember sitting down at the end of every month and trying to make sense of the figures in front of me. It was always exasperating and wearisome. No matter how hard I tried to make things work, something would turn up that would disturb my whole budget.

Until, I finally paid off my monthly mortgage, it felt like a drain on my soul and energy.

I am sure that many people can relate to this feeling.

Mortgage is a painful but unavoidable reality of our life. Most of us have to take some sort of loan to get our dream house or car. In such a case, getting into a mortgage is easy but taking it to full term is not. Month after month is an ordeal.

Having experiences this ordeal first hand, I put together this book. This book is a comprehensive guide that can help you avoid the hassle that comes with a mortgage.

Most mortgage help books that I read were filled with market jargon and economic terms that I didn't understand. Hence I have made a conscious effort to write this book in lay man terms so that everyone can understand the implications of mortgage and how to get rid of them.

From selecting a suitable plan to following it to its successful completion, this book has you covered!

So click the download button right there to

end your financial misery right now!

The curse of interest

Different people have different priorities in life. There is nothing wrong with that. Just different approaches to the way we want to live our lives. Some of us prefer a secure lifestyle with a home of our own, a reasonable car and some emergency savings. There are also those who prefer to live on the edge. Not saving and worrying about the future but rather living in the moment.

There is some advantage to both of these approaches. It makes sense that one should secure the vitals, the basics before moving on to luxuries. There is also no denying that working like a slave for the future takes away the best years of your life. This is the reason, that most of us want a middle ground. The best of both worlds. Though it is easier said than done.

An average person like you and me has a limited income and unlimited desires. The people who run the market, who are in charge of the economy are smart. They recognized this trait early on and hence the concept of lending, borrowing or credit purchases were born.

No matter what name you choose to give to them, at the end of the day, all of these are the same. You are taking someone else's money to fulfill your imminent desires. In return, they get more than what they originally lent on the form of added interest.

These desires can be anywhere from buying a new dress to owning a house. The concept of credit payments allows you to have more items (which in turn means that more desires are fulfilled) than your net income allows.

On the surface, it seems like a genius idea. You no longer have to wait for your paycheck to buy the television set that is now on promotion. You can simply make the purchase against your credit card and take the item home. Easy!

Only it is not so easy. The television is just a simple example. Assume that it retails for $800 on promotion. For an item of those specifications, it is a steal. The only trouble is that you don't have spare $800 to pay for it at that time. So you either choose to pay for it in installments or allow the bank to pay for it for you and then pay the bank in installments.

It is like borrowing money from a friend to pay them back later. The only issue is that this "friend" is demanding more money than they originally lent you.

Most credit cards operate at 15 % annual rate. This can obviously vary according to your personal card plan. This is just as an example. This means that if you take a year to pay back the bank the $800, you will have to pay $920 instead. $120 being interest. The sooner you pay, the lesser your interest will be because most banks add interest additions per month.

Now how does this example of the television concern us?

It concerns us because house mortgages operate in the same manner. It's just that the total amount is much larger.

Just like in the case of the television, it is not the original sum that is a cause of worry. You have to pay it anyway. You owe it. It is the additional interest that is the actual problem. The longer you wait, the more interest will add up. If you decide to pay back the $800 of television within a month, then you will only have to pay $10 extra but the longer you wait, the more sum gets add up.

This is the reason that it is extremely important to get rid of your mortgage as soon as possible. The longer you wait, the more you

extend, the more trouble you'll be in
financially.

Later on in the chapters, we'll talk about
minimizing the time and the damage from the
curse of interest.

Picking the right plan

There is an old saying that the fate of the blow

is decided at the time that the knight lifts his

arm. Half the battle is already won (or lost) even before the blow is stricken.

This couldn't be true. The beginnings are always the most important in everything that you want to do. People say that all's well that ends well but I believe that all's well that begins well. Especially in the case of a home loan.

In today's market driven world, most people enter their adulthood (early 20s) with huge dreams. The dream of having a lush home, a fancy car and an enviable lifestyle. There is nothing wrong with dreaming. In fact, the dreams are what keep us going. However, once you enter the practical life, you realize that achieving this dream is far more difficult than you initially thought. Market prices are rising every day, wages are low, work is tedious and you barely get by with your monthly expenses. This is a bleak picture but it is a truthful one.

However with home loans and car leases, this dream is within the reach of the average person but there is again the problem of the interest. Unless you have enough saved up to actually buy a house with full payment, there is very little that you can do to avoid interest altogether. It is so inter woven with our economic system that it is pretty much impossible to avoid it altogether. Saving up to actually buy a house in full payment can take years and years.

I really don't need to sit here and talk to you about the importance of owning your own house. It is the biggest security umbrella (both literally and figuratively) that you can have. When you have your own house, you'll know that no matter how the circumstances are, you'll at least always have a roof over your head. If you have a family and children, this security becomes even more important.

Due to this, getting your own house should be amongst your top priorities. Above any other material dream that you might have. Having your own modest house is way more important than have a enviable vehicle to drive or designer label clothes to wear.

For a 9 to 5 worker, achieving this security and peace of mind is not possible without interest. You cannot avoid it altogether but what you can do is that you can select a plan that suits your needs the best.

The home loan/money lender market has become competitive. There are many investors who are willing to put their money into this business. This has benefited the average consumer like you and me immensely. As a response to competition, mortgage interest rates are lower and there is more leniency for the borrower.

Due to competition, there are also varying types of plans. Some of them are more popular than the others but just because something is popular doesn't mean that it is also right for you.

Paying off your mortgage without undue mental stress and tension is possible if you select the plan that suits your need. Given below are a few pointers that can help you figure out your preferences and select a plan according to them.

→ Study your credit score

Before you actually apply to a bank or a lender, study your own credit score with an objective eye. If you were a lender, would you lend money to someone with a record like yours? If the answer is yes, then you are ready to move ahead.

To get your mortgage approved, you need a stable income, some down payment money in your account and a clean track record in the past. However if you are self employed or run your business, then it might take some persuasion.

Set your credit score right before you even begin to apply for a mortgage.

→ Amount of Down Payment

Generally the most popular option for down payment is anywhere between 15 - 20 % of the total amount. This is a good enough option that is safe but not necessarily the best. If you are just starting out in life, it is possible that you don't have enough savings to pay 20 % down payment. In such a case, some lenders will allow you a mortgage for as low as 5 %. While this is good for someone starting out and desperate for a home, it is not ideal. The lower your down payment is, the more your interest rate and time of return would be.

If you can give more than 20 % in down payment, then I highly suggest that you do. I know people who bought houses with down payment of as much as 50 %. If you can afford it, is a great move. It will save you much trouble in coming times.

For one, your installments will be lower. Secondly, you can pay off the loan much more quickly.

If you have some funds allocated or stashed somewhere, now is the time to bring them forward. Is there a trust fund you can break? Some jewelry you can pawn? Something else that you can sell to make the down payment?

Select a plan that allows flexible down payment that suits your needs. Try to go as high as you can. I don't suggest draining your bank account entirely but go as high as you possibly can. If you are just starting out, wait a few years and save some money for down payment instead of taking the plunge straight away with as little as 5 % down payment. It will be much better in the longer run.

→ Interest Rate

As a natural instinct, most people are drawn towards the option that gives the lowest interest rates. However, interest rates are not always the best indicator. Lower interest rates often come with hidden charges like bonus payments or mid yearly payments. Make sure that you read and understand everything very clearly before proceeding.

Lower interest rates are also offered if the down payment is large or if the time span is low. If you can manage both of these, then do consider opting for the lowest rates.

→ Time

Time and mortgage are inter related. Some mortgages with small down payment and small installments can go up to 30 years! That is a huge time span. Unless you plan on spending you entire life in that house, don't commit to a plan that is that prolonged.

For example, if you are buying a one bedroom house with a 30 years span, it is not feasible. If you plan on getting married or expanding your family, you will outgrow the house before you have finished paying off for it. As a rule of thumb, your plan should be less than the time you plan on living in the house.

→ Frequency of Payments

Another very important factor that ties up with the interest rate. The more delayed your payments are, the higher will be the interest rate.

However, choose a frequency that you can easily pay. Mostly, you'll have to strike a compromise between the amount and the time but a general rule to follow is to keep the frequency as high as possible.

You studied your credit history in the first step. How much money can you spare for mortgage each month?

For example, let's assume that you can give $2400 per month. Now instead of making one payment of $2400, schedule two payments of $1200 every 15 days. It is the same thing financially but it can make a huge difference in your net interest amount.

You don't have to necessarily increase your budge to increase the frequency. Look for a plan that gives you added benefits with the same amount but increase frequency of payments.

→ Amount of Payments

This is the part that worries most people and leads them into making bad mortgage related decisions. Just because your monthly installment is $1000 instead of $1200 doesn't mean that the former is a better deal. I outlined the other factors in the steps above.

A good thing to do is to work backwards. Select an ideal plan and figure out the monthly amount. Then see if you can spare that much money every month by cutting down some expenses here and there. If not, then move onto the next best plan and see if you can accommodate that with your earnings and living cost. Repeat until you find a perfect match. It will be a compromise but higher payments and higher frequency means that you can be over with your mortgage sooner. Time is the key.

→ Total Cost

At the end of the day, you are paying the lender/bank a huge sum of money. Just because you are paying it in small increments doesn't mean that the amount is not huge. Don't just look at your frequency or total time span or amount of payments. Look at a plan that also gives you the best total cost. You don't want a plan that triples the cost of your property so that when a few years later you set out to sell it, you can't even recover your investment. Compare plans according to the total cost and the market value. Select one that is overall beneficial.

When it comes to selecting a mortgage plan, sadly there is no win-win situation. You will have to compromise on some points to gain an advantage at others. Your task is to figure out where you can slack off and where you can't so that you have a plan that suits your needs perfectly.

Picking the right house

We all have wants and then we all have needs.

When it comes to buying a house on home

loan, you should effectively be able to separate the wants from the needs.

Surely, you desire a big 5 bedroom house with a huge backyard and a personal swimming pool but do you really need it? Is it practical for you?

When buying a house, it is not just about the money that you are paying to own it but also the maintenance cost and the taxes. Which means that the bigger the house will be, the more you'll have to spend to keep it in shape. Not the best bargain.

Most of us start out in life single or with a partner at most. Some people do have children by the time they come around to buying a home but it can be safe to say that in majority of cases, the family is quite small. You need a house that is sufficient for your needs but is by no means extravagant. The bigger your house, the higher the rate and more time it will take for you to pay back your loan.

→ Number of Family Members

A house is not a small investment and you don't get around to buying a house every day. So in our minds, it makes sense to get a house that will be sufficient for when our children will have children.

This is the wrong approach!

The house that you are intending to purchase should cover the needs of your present family or any children that you are planning to have within the next five or ten years. Do not plan ahead of that. Even if in the distant future, your house fails to fulfill your needs, you can always sell the house and use that money as a down payment for another bigger house. You are buying property. It's value increases over time.

If you are two partners and plan on having a child, then a modest 3 bedroom house with a kitchen and a living area will be more than sufficient for you. Do not go around to buy a 5 bedroom house when there are only two inhabitants.

→ Lifestyle

Not all houses are built alike. Some have more spacious bedrooms. Some have a large backyard. Some have a huge living room. The size of the house you select should be in accordance with your lifestyle.

Where do you spend most of your time?

Are you a bedroom person? Are you a living room person? Are you an outdoor person?

Your house plan should be in sync with your lifestyle because there is no point paying extra for lavish bedrooms when you don't even spend that much time there.

→ Location

Real estate prices depend upon the property itself as well as the location. Typically, upcoming neighborhoods have cheaper rates than already established colonies. If you look into them, you might be able to get a better deal. Since, the builders/developers are promoting their property, the prices are comparatively low as compared to a highly populated existing area.

There is also the factor of distance of your work place or children's schools from your residence.

Don't just select a location because it's posh or beautiful. Keep in mind the price, the distance you'll have to cover each day and the future prospects. The upcoming neighborhood might seem a little desolate now but in a few years it could be brimming just like any established part of the city.

Have an eye for that and you can get a great deal.

→ Furniture

This might not cross your mind immediately but it is a fact. The larger the house, the more furniture you'll need to fill it up or otherwise you can have some serious echo for a prolonged time. The size your house should be such that you can easily fill it up within a few years. You don't want a huge house with empty bedrooms.

→ Survey Around

See as many houses as you can. It might get tiring but visit new neighborhoods, meet with sellers and attend open houses. The more you'll check around, the more aware you will be of market position. The more aware you are, the better deal you can secure.

Have a mental blueprint of the house you want and then try to match it to a house on sale. You will already have reasonable expectations by following the above points, now you just have to search around enough to find a house that matches them.

→ Stick to your expectations

There will be a difference of opinion over this one and I understand that but my personal advise to you is that stick to your original expectations. In your search, you might come across a house that exceeds your needs but is available at a so-called steal price. This might sound like a good deal but it isn't.

Buying a house is nothing like buying a pair of shoes on sale. Even if it is a good deal, it is still a huge amount of money. The so-called bargain house, though cheap by its standards is probably still way above your original budget. If you decide to go for it with an absurd mortgage plan, life will become very difficult for you.

Hence it is better to stick to what you have in mind. In the earlier chapter, we discussed how you should allocate a budget before you see a plan or a house. Stick to that budget.

If you have selected an appropriate house and a reasonable plan, you won't have a lot of trouble with your home loan and that's the entire point, isn't it? If you begin it right, the journey will be much more smoother.

Every Penny Counts

Paying off a mortgage is like saving. Only the

end savings would be in the form of real estate

property as opposed to bank balance or cash

at hand. Like any savings, paying off a mortgage requires some serious budgeting.

Now that's something that nobody wants to hear. Nobody wants to be told that they have to curtail their expenses or that they cannot buy this and that. In fact, budgeting doesn't have to be such a scary word. Formally or informally, nearly all of us budget.

We go to our jobs, we pay our taxes and then we devise a plan to spend our net income. A normal, average person saves some of it, spends some of necessities (like bills and groceries) and then reserves some for leisure like shopping and going to the movies. You might do this division formally by writing it all down on a paper or you it might be all in your head. Either way, you have formulated a semi-systematic way to spend your earnings.

That my friend is the essence of budgeting.

In the earlier chapter, we discussed how you need to allocate your budget before you even begin to look for a house or a mortgage plan. This serves two purposes. For one, you will know how much funds you have available for other activities. Secondly, it will ensure that your monthly mortgage amount is such that it doesn't affect your life drastically.

When you are trying to pay off a loan, some changes in your life are bound to happen. This is inevitable because a large chunk of your income is going towards something that is not giving you instant gratification. Usually, when you shop and spend some money, you get a kick out of it. Not this one though because it feels more like a burden because you are not getting anything in your hands right away. This can be frustrating and annoying.

For this very reason, it is extremely important that you make a budget. I have discussed some of the steps that you can take to have a hassle free and financially comfortable month (and year).

→ Calculate your income

You might have just one source of income. You might have several. Some of us rely only on our salaries. Some of us also have side ventures. All is okay, as long as money is rolling in.

The first step in making a budget is to lay out all your possible income in front of you. This includes the income of all family members. If your spouse works, his/her income will count as well.

You need to only take into account the net income. The spendable money that you get after tax deduction and everything else. Write it all down clearly on a page. Pull out your bank statements or whatever you need to do. Just have all your incoming money laid out in front of you.

→ Calculate expenses

Very honestly, write down all your expenses
(not including the mortgage yet). This
includes necessities, luxuries and even non
sense spending. Take any sample month and
calculate the expenditures. Again, you might
need a copy of your bank statement for this.

Now, weigh these total expenses against your
total net income that we calculated in the last
step. If your income is more than your
expenses (or even equal to), you are in safe
waters. You don't have to worry about
anything as of yet.

However, if you are running on credit, then it can pose a problem.

→ Clear your credit

Do not go into a mortgage plan without first clearing off all credit. I mentioned in the first chapter that you can give it any name but at the end of the day, mortgage is just a loan. Your credit with bank is also a loan. You don't want to pile loan upon loan.

If you have credit or you have been running on credit, first clear it off. Curtail your expenses for now and clear off all debts. When you enter a mortgage plan, you don't want to be indebted to anyone else.

→ Disable your credit card

This might seem a little extreme but trust me, this is very important. Your credit card is a debt generating machine. When you are in a mortgage plan or planning to go into one, you want to rid yourself of any other debt in your financial life. Hence disabling your credit card will be the smartest move you make.

A credit card is not a necessity. It is just a ploy that makes you spend more money that you have, which is the last thing you want to be doing right now.

Instead shift to a debit card or even a simple ATM card. This way you'll only spend what you have.

→ Add in mortgage

Once you have cleared all credit, take a look at your financials again. Repeat steps 1 and 2 to figure out how much money you will have each month for spending after you deduct the mortgage.

Once you have a solid, net amount, you can adjust your whole budget according to it. It might seem like it is very little at the start because you are used to a different amount but you can work this out! Once you know how much money you have, it becomes easier to spend it accordingly.

→ Make a rough plan

Every month, with your available money, make a rough plan. You don't have to stick to it hard and fast. It will be just an outline that you can follow. You can even allocate percentages instead of whole figures. For example, 40% of your leftover income will go towards groceries and billings. 25% towards buying clothing. 10% towards general entertainment. You get the jest.

You don't have to allocate any percentage to savings. Your mortgage is you savings at this point. Savings in the form of real estate. Though do have a small emergency fund for medical emergencies and so. You can even put as little as $50 a month in it and you will have $600 a year which is enough at the moment.

Once you cut off the mortgage from the start and decide to work with the leftover, life will be much more easier. If you do the opposite and spend first and pay mortgage later than things might get tricky because it is easy to overspend. By budgeting early on and separating the mortgage amount, you will establish a steady lifestyle. You will know what to expect so the mortgage payments will not hit you as hard. Combine that with a suitable plan that saves you money in the long run and you have a winner!

Ingenious ways to save

Once you have your budget in order, you

might find that you have less money to spend

that what you are used to. This is normal and

nothing to fret about. This slightly lesser money doesn't have to compromise your lifestyle and the activities that you enjoy. You just have to keep an open mind and look for alternative options.

We have already done the budgeting part, your mortgage money is set aside so this isn't about saving money to pay that. You are already paying that from your net income. These savings are done so that you can enjoy the activities that you normally enjoy. You don't have to cut down on them just because of your mortgage. The ideas given below allow you to save money in one aspect so that you can fund another aspect of your lifestyle so that the quality of your living doesn't suffer.

→ Have separate bank accounts

This is a step that I highly recommend. Early on, open a separate bank account. As soon as you get your salary, transfer the mortgage amount to the other bank account. Use that account to only pay for your mortgage. Draw money for use from your original bank account. This will prevent you from spending money from your mortgage fund in a moment of weakness. You already won't have any credit card so you can only spend what you have. It is a good idea to only keep the amount that you can actually spend in your account.

This is especially important if you have fortnightly payments (which I highly recommend). In mortgage payment, time equals money. If you lag behind you schedule, it can cost you thousands of dollars in the long run. So separate the money as soon as you get it.

→ Clip coupons

There's this concept that coupon clipping is only for frugal people. This is a misconception. Companies put out coupons because they want you to use them so use them! In today's world of internet, you can find printable coupons and coupon codes by a simple google search. Search around for possible coupons before you go shopping. Even 10% off is something. You can use that savings on something else now that cash is limited.

→ Change your wi-fi plan

Now-a-days, internet is a necessity. It is impossible to go on without internet. Thinking that, most of us opt for unlimited plan because it sounds the best deal. Only that it isn't. Majority of the people use a very limited amount of data per month. You can easily track it and find an average.

In light of that usage average, shift to a limited plan. If someday you have some extra need, you can just go to a cafe that offers free wi-fi and use the internet over there. Even if you save as little as $30-40, you can use those savings to go see a movie every month.

You will have internet access like before and you can also go see a movie every month. Your lifestyle and social life is not compromised.

→ Quit everything that isn't good for your health

Now where does health come in the midst of finances? Well these two are interrelated.

If you smoke, drink or eat an obscene amount of fast food then now might be a time to quit. Both, you body and your finances will thank you.

On an average, a pack of cigarettes can cost about $5. If you smoke a pack a day, then it is $5 a day, $35 a week, $150 a month and $1825 a year.

Now imagine all the things you can get with the excess $18235. You could buy a new flat screen LED television or a DSLR camera. All while steadily paying your mortgage.

This is from just cutting down cigarettes. Now imagine the savings if you stopped overspending on unhealthy takeouts and sodium filled potato chips as well.

Since all these things are bad for your health anyway, you'll be also saving money on medicines and doctor visits. Use your finances to drive you to live a more healthy lifestyle.

→ Buy in bulk

This is common knowledge. Buying in bulk saves you money. Whenever possible, buy large cartons or boxes. If it is something that can rot soon, then find a friend to share the expenses with. Instead of buying two separate individual items, buy in bulk and divide the money. If this other friend of yours is also trying to pay off mortgage then things can work out fantastically.

You can use the saved money to go out for lunch or dinner once a month. Social activity remains enact because you save somewhere else to fund it.

→ Use your own bank's ATM

Again something that is obvious but still a lot of people skip it. When you use another bank's ATM (out of convenience), that bank charges you an extra fee. You can simple save that fee by keeping a track of your own bank's ATM locations and using them instead.

Use the extra saved money to put some gas in your car or for anything else that you might want.

→ Support local economy

Instead of buying from big brand names, choose to give your money to local sprouting businesses. For fresh produce, get in touch with a local farm instead of buying from a supermarket.

Local produce is fresher and cheaper. Plus at the end of the day, you are supporting something at the grass root level. Look for small shops, small businesses and nearby farms. Use the internet to search around and get the best deal. If you find something great, hook all your friends and family to it. Help them save some money too!

It's really simple when you get down to it. Save ingeniously and spend it somewhere else to sustain your lifestyle. The ideas given above are just a few ones to inspire you and guide you in the right direction. There are many different ways. For example, cutting off premium channels or cable in favor of Netflix or taking the tube instead of a single person driving a car all the way across the town. Be aware of hidden charges (like the ATM one) and learn to avoid them. I don't like to call it frugal living as some snobs have named it. I like to call it intelligent spending. After all, why pay more when you can pay less?

Welcoming surprise money

There is a high chance that during the course

of you mortgage payment, you'll come across

money from unexpected sources. It might

happen. It might not happen. Either way, it is better to be prepared.

This money can come in the form of a work bonus, end of year tax returns, inheritance or unexpected gifts.

We earlier discussed how important budgeting is. If you would be sticking to the budget, you might be a little tired of living from pay check to pay check. It is all very understandable.

In the midst of that, if you come across some extra money, it will seem like a great get away. You can use that money for everything! From buying a fancy new dress or enjoying a family evening at a fine restaurant. All of these are viable and understandable plans.

Now I'm going to be a party pooper here and say that you should not indulge these dreams. Before you frown, please at least listen to me.

Before this money came along, you were managing quite fine. Even indulging because of our plan to save here and spend there. Your lifestyle is not largely affected and you are still enjoying life like you always have. More money means more things and more activities. We think that it also means a better life or a more enjoyable time.

Don't sound wary. This is not a philosophy book. I am not going to tell you how money is not linked to happiness etc. Instead, we are going to talk from a practical point of view.

At this stage in life, your first priority is to get out of debt. Wearing a fancy dress or going somewhere comes after that. You have figured this out quite earlier. Hence according to the priority list made by "you", this extra money should go towards paying off your mortgage.

An unexpected high payment can reduce the cost of your other regular payments or end your mortgage term much sooner, depending upon what you choose. If you choose the same time span, your monthly (or fortnightly) installments will reduce. This will leave you with some extra money every month that you can use for indulgence.

If you choose to pay the same amount, the time span of your mortgage will decrease. As I have mentioned countless times, time is money in this case. The sooner you pay off, the lower the interest will be. This means that at the end of the term, you will be saving a lot of money. Won't that be like a bonus?

Most mortgages operate on the policy of compound interest. Which means that the interest will apply on the total remaining amount (including previous added interest) as opposed to the basic initial amount. Due to this, the longer you'll wait, the more money will pile up and the more money you'll have to pay.

When you begin paying mortgage installments, it is probable that you won't touch the base amount for quite long. Month after month, you'll only be paying the added interest. This can be quite frustrating.

In such a case, the unexpected money can come quite in handy. You can use it to make large payments so that you make a dent in your base amount. This way, you'll actually be reducing the core amount. Once you make an initial dent, the following payments will continue to make a difference in your base amount.

It isn't really rocket science.

I can understand that the temptation of spending such money elsewhere would be great but remind yourself why you're doing it all in the first place. You were getting along just fine without a sudden boost to your bank account. Shift the money to your other bank account (reserved for mortgage payment) as soon as your receive it. Treat it like it wasn't even there. At the end, when your mortgage will end sooner and you'll save a lot of money, you'll pat yourself on the back for making the right decision.

Remaining on your toes

It is very easy to just figure out a budget, make payments and forget about the loan altogether apart from the check that you draw every month. This is a no hassle approach and may minimize the stress in your life. However, it is not always the best approach.

Real estate market is a dynamic one. It is not stagnant. Rates and policies change every day. Interest rates could be lower one day and then higher the next day. If you are oblivious to market changes, you might miss a golden opportunity when you are just simply writing check after check.

In the real estate market, awareness and knowledge is the key. It can make all the difference between profit and loss.

I will suggest that keep up with the dynamics of the market at least on a monthly basis. Check the changing trends and see if there is any way that they can benefit you.

Usually as time passes, interest rates climb up. However, in some rare cases, they also come down. This might be due to the inflation in the market or any other plausible reason. If you have a flexible plan, talk to your lender about how it affects you. For the time period, you might be able to snag some low interest rates (it's a huge maybe).

Even if that does not happen, some lenders allow the option of shifting the property. Due to market inflation, prices might be lower than when you initially took the plan. In such a case, you might be able to find an upgraded property at the same rate as you are paying now. Such a shift at the right time can be a huge golden investment in the long run because 15 or 20 years down the lane, the better property will pay you much better rates than when you originally started.

Some lenders charge an extra sum for the shift. Talk to your lender about this and be very clear about the terms. There are some lenders who allow the shift for free or very minimal rates. If your lender is one such person/organization, then talk to them and evaluate your options.

Another scenario can be the rise of prices in the area that you live and inflation in another part of the town. This can also be very beneficial if you are willing to make a change. You can sell your current home at the higher prices and then use that as a down payment for a house in the inflated sector. This way you'll have made a larger down payment and

hence your remaining debt would be lower.
This of course, depends upon the factor
whether you want to make the change or not
but if you do, then it can be very beneficial.

Being aware means that you can save the
maximum amount of money by just doing
some extra reading. Not a bad deal at all.

Increasing your income

Having a debt is equivalent to someone taking

away a large chunk of your income. Even

though, we have talked about ways that can

save you some money, it might also be viable to consider options that can increase your income.

→ Every family member contributes

Paying off mortgage is a family effort. You are all in this together. Hence the burden of payments should not fall upon the shoulders of one person. Find a way by which every single member of the family can contribute to the income. If you have children, they can contribute their small share (not to you but for taking care of their own wants) by babysitting or mowing the lawn and other small jobs.

→ Freelance

You can use your primary job skill to make some extra money at the side. Just make sure that your employer didn't make you sign a non-compete contract. With little effort and some time, you can earn some extra cash while retaining your regular stable job.

For example, if you work in computer section for your day job, you can have a small freelance business at the side of solving software glitches. You'll be surprised to know that so many people don't know a lot about things that you take for granted. Like installing windows (operating system) into computers or correcting hardware installation problems. You can use these skills to your advantage.

→ Write/Blog/Vlog

There is always a market for writing. Whatever job you have during the day, write about it. For example, if you do repairs for a living, you can run a DIY repair blog where you give people tips and tricks. Blogging is a very lucrative business right now. With some flair and authentic knowledge, you can earn a good amount of money via ad placements.

→ Invest

We may not exactly be the <u>wolves of wall street</u> but that doesn't mean that we can't use the stock market to our advantage. With a little knowledge and a slow start, you can have a good turnover with little investment and even little effort. It is worth checking at the least.

→ Rent

The most obvious for the last.

If you have a large space or even a bedroom that you don't use, you can rent it. If you live in a college town, you can rent your bedroom to a single student. It can make you some extra money on the side.

If you have a larger space, you can rent your basement or your top floor to some small family without affecting your own living. This way you can use your property to generate some money while you are paying off its mortgage.

Renting doesn't have to be limited to house space. You can pretty much rent everything. From your car to book to your home theatre. There is somebody who needs these things but doesn't want to buy them. You just have to get in touch with them. Use the internet to your advantage for this.

Again, the ideas given above are just a few examples. There are endless ways to make some side money with little to no effort, you just have to be creative. Making extra money doesn't always mean doing extra shifts. Just look around for an opportunity and grab onto it. Even an extra $100 are something.

Conclusion

Thank you for reading this book.

I hope that you found it of help.

Mortgage is a pressing reality of today's times. No matter who you are or what you do, chances are that you need some kind of loan to make a huge purchase. In that case, mortgage comes to your rescue.

Only that mortgage can be more of a mental stress than any source of relief. This can take a toll on your mental health. Hence I wrote this book to relieve some of that strain.

With the right approach and guidance, you can sail through the mortgage years with ease and have it off your back within a few years.

Pen Paper Thankyou by Geralt

Finally, if you enjoyed this book, then I'd like

to ask you for a favor, would you be kind

enough to leave a review for this book on Amazon? It'd be greatly appreciated!

Thank you and good luck

Living Well,

Spending Less

The Ultimate Planner To Help

You Discover An Enjoyable

Life While Living Well and

Spending Less

K. ELIZABETH

©2016

Table of Contents

Introduction

"Money has never made man happy, nor will it, there is nothing in its nature to produce happiness. The more of it one has the more one wants."

-Benjamin Franklin

Societies around the world have adopted and continue to adopt the idea that wealth is synonymous with happiness. We oftentimes believe that the purchase of a shiny, new luxury SUV will satisfy our desire for fulfillment. We spend our paychecks on the latest technology or high-end fashion because we equate our status in the technological and fashion world with our own happiness. Sure, this works for some. Perhaps the thought of driving your new luxury car to work *really does* make the thought of your stressful 9-5 work day a less dreadful prospect. Maybe keeping up with the latest fashion trend *really does* increase your happiness because you feel confident, beautiful, and successful in the clothes you wear.

But if we embrace this "money-leads-to-happiness" mindset, what happens when we simply can't budget that new car or carve time out of our busy work schedules for weekend shopping? Does the amount of money in our bank account mean we can't live well and be happy? Of course not. Contrary to the increasingly popular belief that money means happiness, we can still live highly enjoyable lives without breaking our bank account. What's more, we can continue to live equally enjoyable lives while also spending less in the process. A few budget and lifestyle tweaks may be in order depending on your current situation, but, as you'll soon discover, these tweaks are, well, tweaks—they're minor changes to your daily routine.

Regardless of your age, gender, race, or geological location, this book is for you. Whether you're a hardworking single parent, a dedicated working professional, a struggling college student, an aspiring artist, or a driven entrepreneur, living well while spending less won't require drastic life changes or long-term efforts.

Chapter 1: What Kind of Spender Are You?

Spending less is all about making tweaks to our daily routine and lifestyle. But in order for us to accomplish these changes, we first need to identify the areas that need changing in the first place, right?

Quiz

We oftentimes need to reflect on our hobbies and habits in order to recognize where exactly our money is going and how we can reduce our spending. But for this to happen, we need to know exactly what questions to ask ourselves—this can be hard to do, especially when we don't want to hear our own answers. So, we've created this quiz to get you moving in the right direction. Take some time to answer the questions that follow, and do so as *honestly* as you can. Fibbing about your spending habits during this self-reflection quiz won't do you any good in the later chapters.

1. *You are hosting a few close friends at your house tonight. Do you:*

A. Ask everyone to bring something?

B. Fill a few bowls with chips and prepare small finger-food plates?

C. Buy a few cases of beer and/or a few bottles of wine?

D. Order Chinese take-out.

2. *Check off which money-managing description best fits your lifestyle:*

A. People ask me for money advice.

B. I have a budget and plan my spending in advance.

C. I check my bank account once a week.

D. I don't keep track of my spending.

3. *While out shopping you:*

A. Purchase the cheapest thing you *need.*

B. Write a list but sometimes depart from it.

C. Shop with an idea of what you want in mind but don't look at the cost.

D. Buy whatever you want.

4. *By the end of the weekend, you:*

A. Know your account balance and have already budgeted for next week.

B. Have a general idea of what you spent the previous week.

C. Had to borrow some money from family or friends.

D. Have no idea how much you have in your account.

5. *When you go out with friends you:*

A. Actually, you rarely go out except for special occasions.

B. Use your "night-out" budget and stick to it.

C. Try to go to places with good deals, but don't stress if you don't.

D. Like to splurge and go wherever your friends want to go.

6. *Choose what you most enjoy:*

A. Saving your money. You feel guilty spending your money.

B. Spending your money on items you know you'll get your money's worth for.

C. Spending money on items you pass by in a store.

D. Retail therapy and weekend shopping trips.

7. What does the majority of your money go towards?

A. Bills, grocery, and necessities, ugh.

B. Your savings account.

C. A split between necessities and things I just want.

D. Keeping up with the latest technology, décor, and fashion trends.

Interpreting your results

- **Mostly As:** You're *very* aware of your budget and do everything you can to limit and even eradicate your spending. But it still seems that you're not able to do and buy the things you *want*. Keep reading. This book will show you some simple ways to save and earn money while also indulging in the things you otherwise might not be able to. We recommend paying special attention to:

    o **Chapters** 2, 5, and 6

- **Mostly Bs:** Answering mostly Bs indicates that you have a bit of monetary flexibility, but that you're still very conscious of your bank account activity and what you spend. It would seem you're on the cusp of being able to spend money on the things you want, but that you often shy away from doing so. No worries, this book will help get you over that sometimes intimidating line. We recommend paying special attention to:
  - **Chapters** 2, 4, and 5
- **Mostly Cs:** It seems you're in a pretty decent financial position. You don't fear

the thought of an empty bank account, you're not restricted from enjoying the things you love, and you may even have the opportunity to unguiltily splurge on the things you want. While spending less money may not be a pressing concern for you, you'll still find great ideas in this book that will help you put *more* money toward the things you enjoy most. We recommend reading:

- o **Chapters** 4, 6, and 7
- **Mostly Ds:** You've got a wide range of monetary freedom and flexibility. Your bank account isn't a restraint for you

and you're fortunate enough to indulge in luxuries without worry. Spending less money may not be a great concern for you, but it might still be something you're interested in—spending less money while maintaining your lifestyle will let you indulge even *further* in the things you favor most. You might find these chapters of interest:

- **Chapters** 3, 4, and 7.

Chapter 2: Cutting Down on Food Expenses

Depending on the size of your family, a large portion of your money probably goes toward food, whether it's takeout food, restaurant food, fast food, or school snacks for the kids. But hopefully you're already seeing a trend—there's *a lot* of different food options out there. Fortunately, there's an equal amount of ways *anyone* can cut their food expenses in half.

Store-bought vs. takeout

Whether you're a single parent in America or a working professional in France, the thought of takeout food can be an incredibly tempting idea after an exhaustively long day. But keep in mind that while takeout, restaurant, and fast food are oftentimes hassle free, their costs generally rack up faster than store-bought food. Here's why:

1. Eating out at Outback Steakhouse:

- Classic Grilled Chicken: 8 oz. grilled chicken topped with a Cabernet sauce and served with mashed potatoes and a broccoli garnish.

- *Cost:*
  - $13.99 (does not include tax, drink, or tip).
  - With tip: $16.00 (20%)

2. Cooking the same meal at home:

- Home-made chicken dish: 8 oz. grilled chicken served with mashed potatoes and steamed broccoli.
  - *Cost breakdown:* (We averaged the cost of each cooking material

and then found the total cost for 1

serving).

- 1 8 oz. chicken breast: $1.50

- 3-4 medium potatoes: $.50

- 1 pound of broccoli: $1.80

  (you'll have leftovers, too)

- Total: $3.80

Sure, it's nice to sit down, wind down, and let

someone else cook for you after a long day, but

at what cost? A chicken dish at Outback

Steakhouse will cost you $16.00 whereas less

than an hour of your time cooking the same

plate will cost you nearly a fourth. That's a

huge difference.

UK food vendors have recently introduced a product called "Ugly Boxes." They're filled with fresh fruits and vegetables that vendors don't want to buy because they aren't the perfect shape. You can get a box filled with 20-30 delicious fruits and vegetables for about 2 UK pounds ($3.00 USD). Browse the internet to see if an Ugly Box supplier is located near you.

Cutting your weekly grocery bill in half

If we've successfully swayed you into cooking more meals from home, then you're next step will be to learn how to cut your grocery bill in half. But rest assured, this doesn't mean you need to cut the amount of food you buy in half, too. Actually, it's all about planning ahead and shopping at the right time.

- **Freeze them 'til you need them:** Certain foods can be frozen until you need them, so if there's a deal, take it. Let's say butter normally cost $3.90 but it's on sale for $2.00. Buy a few boxes and freeze them until you need them.

- **Buy store brand:** Store brand products are *always* cheaper than brand-name products, yet they contain almost identical nutrients and ingredients. It's the same product and quality; brand-name products are simply more expensive because they're advertised.

- **Have a list and budget:** Know how much money you have to spend and exactly what you need *before* you enter a grocery store—it'll keep you from overspending. Create a list, set a budget, and stick to it.

  o **Bonus tip:** never grocery shop on an empty stomach—*everything* will look delicious and you *will*

justify needing more than you
actually do.

- **Use what you already have:** Check
your cabinets before you spend money
on ingredients you already own. If your
cabinets are full but you're not sure what
to make with your ingredients, try using
All recipes or **Super cook.** These
apps let you enter the ingredients you
have in your cabinet and tell you what
meals you can make from them and how
much cooking time they require.

- **Learn to love leftovers:** You might
need to spend $20 buying ingredients

needed to make vegetarian lasagna in a 13x9 pan, but you'll have leftovers that will feed a family of 4 for at least 2 more meals. If we think about it this way, a large serving of lasagna only costs about $1.50.

Chapter 3: Adopting a Minimalist Mindset

Like we mentioned in the introduction, many societies tend to favor the extravagant and luxurious. Unfortunately, not everyone can live a lifestyle like that. Actually, most of the *world's* population can't. That's why it's crucial we embrace and adopt a minimalist mindset, especially if we want to spend less money while simultaneously enjoying the life we live. But don't worry, this isn't as hard as it sounds.

Minimalist mindsets

Embracing a minimalist mindset—appreciating life's simplicities and the things we already or naturally possess—is a guaranteed way to reduce your monetary spending and increase your well-being and personal *mental* and *emotional* wealth. For example, a minimalist might appreciate nature's beauty. Instead of spending hundreds of dollars on a landscape painting, a minimalist would take a walk or hike in the nearby forest, field, or hiking path. You'll see the same beauty you can find in a painting, except the only difference is that it's free.

If you're motivated and dedicated to doing some self-reflection and perspective modifying, take some time to read the following elements of minimalism. You might come to discover that adopting a minimalist mindset isn't as hard as you thought.

- **Make Reductions:** This doesn't mean throw anything and everything that you love out of your life. It simply means cutting back on the nonessentials—this can happen at whatever pace you feel comfortable with. So, let's say you love collecting antique books, though they can be rather pricey. If you generally buy 10 antique books per month, try buying only 9 the following month, 8 the next month, and so on. You can still purchase them from time to time, but taking on this minimalist mindset will encourage you to see antique book-buying as a treat, not a habit.

- **Find happiness with what you have:** Sometimes it's easier said than done, but it's not impossible. Find free or natural things in your life that you appreciate or love, then focus on them. You'll likely find that you won't need other things (and therefore won't need to spend money) when you come to recognize the importance of what you already have.

- **Simplicities make for an easier life:** It's true. The less things you have, the easier life typically is. If you don't own an expensive boat, you don't need to dish out money every year for cleaning, maintenance, and storage. Likewise, a smaller house requires less cleaning than a mansion. If you embrace this minimalist logic, you'll find that you no longer crave the luxurious and potentially headache-inducing items you once did.

Adopting minimalist elements into your own life

Applying these minimalist mindsets doesn't have to be a one-day thing, nor should it. Actually, you'll find that a slow transition into these three minimalist mindsets or perspectives works best. Here's an example of what we mean:

Making minimalist reductions to your daily routine

Embracing a minimalist mindset is important because it *will* help you spend less money while also living a lifestyle you still enjoy. Furthermore, we want to show you just how easy it is to apply these minimalist mindsets to your daily life. So here's a realistic example many of us can relate to: let's say you drink *a lot* of coffee throughout your day. Maybe you drink one cup of home-brewed coffee before leaving the house, buy one from Dunkin Donuts on the way to work, purchase a cup on your lunch break from a local café, and then treat yourself to a Starbucks mocha latte on your way home. On average, that's about $10 **a day** in coffee, or, $50 **per work week**— there's definitely some room for reduction here. To reduce your coffee intake, you might try the following:

Monday: Replace your morning Dunkin Donuts coffee with another cup of your home-brewed coffee in a travel mug. A small coffee from Dunkin Donuts will cost you about $1.50 while a home-brewed coffee will be about $.10 a cup.

Tuesday: Do the same as you did on Monday, but this time, you should also replace your afternoon cup of coffee with a cup of tea. You'll still get the caffeine you crave, but your bag of tea will cost about $.5.

Wednesday: Follow *both* Monday and Tuesday's suggestions.

Thursday: Continue to replace your afternoon cup of coffee with tea. However, limit your morning home-brewed coffee to only one cup. It's a small difference, but you'll save about $.10 a day doing so.

Friday: You might be in a good mood because it's Friday, so skip that evening cup of coffee from Starbucks altogether. You'll save about $2.00 a day/$10.00 a week by doing so.

Saturday: Maybe you won't be doing as much running around today, so try to limit yourself to only 1 cup of home-brewed coffee throughout the entire day. If you desperately need some caffeine, boil some water and make yourself a cup of caffeinated tea instead.

Sunday: If you've followed the above schedule, you're ready to give up coffee altogether. It's okay to treat yourself every once and a while to a brand-name coffee, but stick to the caffeinated tea. It'll do the same thing as coffee, but you'll save tons of money in the process. How much you ask? Take a look:

If the average cup of coffee from Dunkin Donuts (USA), Starbucks (USA, UK), Costa Coffee (UK), Lavazza Coffee (Italy), Tim Hortons (Canada), Gloria Jean's (Australia), and McCafe (global) costs about $2.00 (USD) and you follow the above example, you'll save:

- $10.00 **a day**
- $50 **a week** (Monday-Friday)

- $200 **a month**

- $600 **in 3 months**

- $1,200 **in 6 months**

- $2,400 **in one year** (crazy, we know).

Chapter 4: Earn and Save Money

For some people, spending less money but living the same lifestyle is an easy task to accomplish. For others, the goal of spending less money is easier said than done. We know that living *does* cost money. We also know that some individuals and families are *already* spending as little as possible but still struggle to get by. That's why we've added in the following 2 chapters. Sometimes, spending less money while living a lifestyle you want just isn't an option—but earning and saving money is while you do this can be.

Earn money using a computer or app

Fortunately, technology provides us with some really great ways to earn money quickly and easily. If you have access to the internet and have items hanging around your house or apartment that you no longer need or use, then the following suggestions might be good for you:

- **OfferUp:** This buying and selling outlet can be accessed by an internet browser or downloaded as an app on any somewhat recent android and iOS phone. If you're familiar with Craigslist and eBay, OfferUp is kind of like combining the two. If you're not familiar with these older online bartering sites, OfferUp allows sellers (you) to upload and post pictures of the item(s) you wish to sell. What you choose to sell is entirely up to you—buyers look for anything, really—from furniture to antiques, from dirt-bikes to clothes. There are no fees because you must meet with people (usually in safe public places) in your area to exchange items for cash. You can direct message with buyers to set up meeting times, and the site/app is extremely easy to navigate.

- **Close5:** Close5 is another *free* app that allows users to log in through their Facebook or create an account, all within 30 seconds. You'll be able to quickly and easily post classified local aids for essentially any item you wish to sell. And as a plus, you need only upload a picture of the item you want to sell—no description, no hassle. Close5 targets buyers and sellers within a 5 mile radius, which makes this app essential to sellers who have limited or unreliable transportation. The only drawback is that Close5 is only supported within the United States, at least for now.

Earn money the good ol' fashion way

Even if you don't have access to the internet or you simply aren't as technologically-savvy, there are still some really productive and simple ways to earn a little money on the side:

- **Yard Sale:** If you have some free time, patience, and nice weather, having a yard/garage sale is a great way to earn some extra cash: you don't need transportation—you can do it in your driveway or front yard—and it's free. Advertising is free, too. All you need is some cardboard and markers to make signs to hang around the neighborhood. Yard sales are also great because they can be quite surprising—what you see as trash might be an antique to someone else. With some bartering skills and patience, anyone and *everyone* is guaranteed to earn some extra money to put toward their savings.

Save money

The thought of saving money can sometimes seem like an overwhelming process, especially if you don't have a large income in the first place. For some, the thought of depositing even $50 a month into a savings account can be a financial burden. Fortunately, there are a plethora of simple ways you can save your money without really noticing you're missing it. Interested? Keep reading.

The 52-week saving challenge

Yes, saving money over the course of a year can seem like a looming and long-winded process, but by the end of the 52 weeks, you'll have saved over $1,000—$1,352 to be exact. The best part is that you'll save all this money while barely noticing a change in your bank account. Here's how:

Essentially, each week you should add $1 more than the previous week. Here's what it looks like on paper:

Week	Deposit	Balance
Week 1	$.50	$.50
Week 2	$1.50	$2.00
Week 3	$2.50	$4.50
Week 4	$3.50	$8.00
....	....	....
Week 51	$50.50	$1,300.50
Week 52	$51.50	$1352.00

If you're beginning to hyperventilate at the thought of adding upwards of $40.00 each week to your saving account, don't. Add what you can, but try to meet your weekly goal. If following this just isn't a possibility, however, don't fret. Just by looking at Weeks 1-4 you can easily see how quickly your money adds up. So if you can only contribute, say, $10 a week to your saving challenge, do that. In a year you'll have saved $520.

Helpful hint: Are you still stressing about this challenge? Remember in chapter 3 when we demonstrated how reducing your daily coffee intake alone can save you money? (If you typically drink 3 cups of chain-bought coffee a day, eliminating your intake will save you about $6.00 a day, which adds up to

$30.00 a week.) Cut the caffeine and put the money toward this challenge instead. You'll thank yourself for doing so in a year, we promise.

Chapter 5: Free Knowledge

Like we briefly mentioned in the last chapter, sometimes spending less money doesn't *completely* do the trick. To best live the happy and well life we deserve, we sometimes need to do more than spend less money—based on our financial situations, we may need to spend less money *and* increase our income. Using our existing knowledge, learning new skills, and applying it to income-producing activities is a great remedy. Although you should actively work toward spending less money, having a side income is always a great approach to living well and maintaining what you deem to be an acceptable lifestyle. Fortunately, there's a plethora of **free** resources out there that will supply you with the knowledge and skills you need in order to earn an additional income.

Learning new skills from free resources

If you have access to the internet, the following have the potential to be invaluable resources. You can watch step-by-step videos on how to create essentially *anything* you can think of, or you can learn an entirely new skill by the simple click of a button and some of your time. Plus, they're all free.

- **YouTube:** It's free, easy to use, and always at your fingertips. As long as you have a search keyword in mind, you should be able to find whatever you're looking for. It's also an excellent resource for fostering or expanding your knowledge because it's video format appeals to multiple learning styles, primarily visual and auditory learners (Visual learners understand by seeing and auditory learners understand by hearing). How-to videos *almost always* include both. If you want to learn to crotchet, for example, so that you can sell scarves, hats, and mittens as a side income, YouTube is a perfect match. Simply searching "how to crotchet" will lead you to thousands of free step-by-step videos.

- **Online courses:** Free online courses can be a bit tricky to find, but they're definitely out there. They're often easy to navigate, clearly organized, and more importantly, typically let you learn and progress at your own pace, so they're absolutely worth the time you spend looking for them.

- **Webinars:** For those less technology-savvy, webinars are seminars that are conducted over the internet. It's very much like sitting in a class listening to a teacher talk or lecture. If you're looking for additional guidance or a social element, you may want to look into webinars over online courses. Both are great, but webinars oftentimes allow you to communicate with your teacher or leader via video chats. You usually have ample opportunities to ask questions, which is crucial when you're learning and practicing new skills that you plan to earn an income from.

Additional free resources

There are just too many resources out there that give you the opportunity to expand your knowledge without paying a cent, so we simply can't explain them all. However, the following is a great—and we mean *great*—list of additional **free** resources you can consult and take advantage of as you seek ways to earn an income. Here's a helpful link where you can find many of the following resources explained in more detail:

❖ http://www.iflscience.com/technology/take-college-and-university-courses-online-completely-free

And here's the list of additional free resources:

- **Coursera:** the most popular world-wide online education facilitator available in 12 different languages.
- **Edx:** another highly recommended resource that offers free online classes

(It was founded by Harvard and MIT partners, so you know it's great).

- **MIT:** Yes, one of the world's best schools has made available—completely free—most of the teaching materials that can be found on campus or in the MIT library.

- **Duolingo:** An app must-have for anyone seeking to learn or brush up on a language.

For those less technologically-savvy...

No need to worry if you don't feel comfortable using the internet or don't have access to the internet. There are still some really great options available to those hoping to learn or improve a skill for profit. Two great learning/practicing a skill options are:

- **Joined groups:** Essentially, a joined group consists of a group of people who generally meet once or twice a week to learn and practice a particular skill(s). This resource is great, not only because it's free and you get to socialize, but also because you'll learn unique and invaluable skills from those around you. Your unique approach to a certain skill might be the flare your work needs to sell and earn you an income.

- **Your local library:** Sure, checking a book out from the library might seem "old-school," but the library is extremely underrated. It's filled with how-to books that will get your independent business or income-earning hobby on its feet, not to mention you're surrounded by books written by credible and highly educated sources.

Chapter 6: Travel More, Spend Less

When we think about spending less money, we sometimes think it means we can no longer go on our usual vacations or treat ourselves to fun activities. Fortunately, spending less money *isn't* a prison sentence. With the help of some really fantastic travel apps that offer competitive daily discounts, you'll be able to take your family on your annual summer vacation or indulge in a spa-day with friends without feeling guilty about it.

Groupon

There are so many great things we love about Groupon. First and foremost, it's a free downloadable app available for both android and iOS devices—you can also access it via the internet on a computer, cell phone, or tablet. It's available in hundreds of cities across the world, which makes it an extremely accessible app. By entering your location and a search keyword (if you have something specific in mind), you'll be brought to an easily navigable page that displays daily local deals and discounts, consisting of anything, really—

discounts at restaurants, spas, hotels, shopping vouchers, things to do, and international travel/vacation are all at your fingertips. Most deals have a wide range of date options so you won't be confined to a specific date, which is great for the working individual or family who can't easily take off work.

If money is extremely tight—as in you're barely scrapping by in paying your bills—even the fantastic daily discounts Groupon has to offer may not be a responsible choice. However, if you've followed the 52 week money-saving challenge outlined in Chapter 4, you deserve to treat yourself to a vacation. Here's why:

If you followed the 52 week challenge, you've now saved $1,352. Let's say you've decided to use half of your savings ($650) to treat you and your partner to a tropical vacation. With Groupon, a couple with a $650 budget can:

- Stay at a 4 star all-inclusive Cancun, Mexico resort (airfare included) for 4 nights. ($649).

Or, if you have a family of 5 and want to use only $100 of your savings to treat your family to a fun, rainy-day, indoor activity, you can:

- Treat the entire family to 2 sessions of Monster Mini Golf ($20 each, but they're normally $40.)

Remember, spending less money doesn't always mean you need to sacrifice your much-needed vacation time or limit the fun activities you do as a family. Yes, the goal is to spend less money, but actively earning and saving money on the side will absolutely give you some much-needed flexibility to do the things you *want*. The task of spending less money will seem less dreadful if you allow yourself a budget for the occasional individual or familial splurge. For most financial situations, your social or entertainment life doesn't have to end when cutting back on expenses.

Further suggestions

If you have something specific in mind—a day trip to Roger William's Zoo or an all-inclusive hiking tour to Machu Picchu, for example— Groupon sometimes doesn't offer exactly what you're looking for. Fortunately, there are plenty of other great discount websites and apps that you can take advantage of if you're in a stable financial situation and are able to budget responsibly and reasonable. Any of the following helpful sites work the same way as Groupon does, but they oftentimes have different offers going on:

- **Living Social:** This is Groupon's biggest competitor, and for good reason. You can easily find local, daily, and instant deals by entering your location and a keyword, if you have one in mind. If you can't find it on Groupon, we highly suggest looking for it here.

- **Yipit:** This resource is very similar to Living Social and Groupon—you search by keyword and are given a multitude of discounted deals that pertain to your search keyword. But unlike its competitors, Yipit allows users to pay for the deals or services they receive *after* they receive them, not before. So if you know you're getting a bonus from work next week but want to book your vacation or activity now, you can. It's a great feature because you oftentimes have to move fast with these types of discounted deals.

Conclusion

The decision to cut back on expenses can sometimes be a hard one, though it doesn't have to be. With a few simple yet highly effective tweaks to your current lifestyle, you'll noticeably reduce your spending without noticing a drastic shift in your lifestyle. From discovering the shocking expense difference between eating out or eating in and learning how to cut your grocery costs by noticeable amounts, you'll cut your food costs without sacrificing quality or quantity. You've learned the effectiveness of adopting a minimalist mindset in order to decrease spending, but you've also been introduced to money-earning and saving methods that will support you as you work toward spending less money. Furthermore, you now have access to free yet highly recommended resources that will help improve your already existing skills or foster new knowledge in a hobby or activity that can provide you with a side income as you work toward limiting your spending. And lastly, you've got a few new apps to browse next time you're able to budget a family vacation or a fun day trip—just be financially responsible and reasonable about it. And remember, spending less money **doesn't** mean you need to sacrifice your happiness or lifestyle. Follow the previous suggestions, try your hand at income-producing hobbies, and treat yourself to the occasional splurge without guilt. When you make spending less money a less dreadful decision, you'll find that it becomes a much easier process.

Living Well, Spending Less

Enforcing a Successful Spending Ban - Confessions, Tips and Motivation from a Recovering Shopaholic

K. ELIZABETH

©2016

Introduction

I remember the time. Clearly. Vividly.

I would get this feeling. In my gut. It would be almost like a tingling sensation in my hand. The sensation, the want to spend some money and to bring home something that I didn't really need.

I also remember the times when I would see something. In a magazine, in a store display or in an advertisement and I would not be able to get it out of my head. It got so bad that it would even haunt my dreams.

Does it sound like your life story to you?

Well then you have come to the right place. Having struggled with a compulsive shopping problem for years, one day I decided enough was enough. I was running out of space, my finances were low and it was more trouble than it was worth. I took the decision and I pulled through. However the journey had not been easy.

Realizing that, I decided to put together this book to help out my fellows who are struggling out there. Having suffered personally, this book is a very up close and personal account of how to enforce a spending ban so that you can achieve some peace of mind. I have included all the tips, tricks and shortcuts that I found helpful and I am sure that you will find them helpful as well.

If you are sick, tired and frustrated of your impulse purchases and want to stop right now, then get this book and take your first step towards a life of healing, happiness and prosperity.

Table of Contents

HOW TO OWN LESS BUT LIVE MORE?

CONCLUSION

Why do I feel the compulsive need to shop?

Let's imagine a scenario.

You are sitting in your home, changing television channels, flipping through a magazine or even petting your dog. It could be a lazy Sunday. It could be the evening of a workday. All of a sudden, well not really sudden but the feeling arises in your heart. You wish to go browse the racks, to look at stuff, smell the new things and come back laden with shopping bags.

Soon enough, the air of your home or your room becomes stifling and you wish to step out. To get in your car and drive (or walk) to the nearby mall. You also have some makeshift partially legitimate reason for your trip.

"Oh, I'm just going to get some bread"

"Oh, I need to buy a jar of jam"

But it is never about the jam or the bread? Is it? You go for the bread or the jam and come back with hundred other things including clothes, gadgets, cosmetics, crockery and other hoard of things that neither you nor anyone in your house needs.

I can almost see you smiling.

I know that it has happened to you. It might even be a common occurrence but how do I know?

Simply because I have done it as well!

I have no qualms in accepting that I'm a recovering shopaholic. Now when I say recovering, I take this term very seriously. Almost as if someone was recovering from a drug addiction. Just like a whiff tempts the former addict, the hoard of goods also tempt me. They tempt me to swish out my credit card and swipe it without having a second thought but I resist because now I know better.

Before, we go into the details of the recovery, it is first important to understand the reasons that give air to a shopping addiction in the first place. Just like any other addiction, shopping addiction also has deep roots within your mind and psyche. You just don't wake up one day and go around giving tons of profit to the shops in your town. It is a slow and gradual process and it is often helped along by triggers.

Prior to finding a solution to any problem, it is first important to understand the problem. You have termites in your house and you need to get rid of them. Before you start the ridding process, you need to understand where the termites are coming from so that you can cut them off from the base and not just treat the surface.

Dealing with compulsive shopping is no different. Unless you understand the reasons that compel you, simply treating the surface won't do any good.

For example, one thing that a lot of people do is that they disable their credit card or not keep a lot of cash at hand in a false attempt to treat their problem. While it may stop them for some time, it is not a satisfactory solution. The problem is not the credit card or the cash. The problem is you! Hence you need to work on yourself, for the sake of your financial as well as mental health.

→ Boredom

Shopping is not just a need based activity for a lot of people (including myself). It is also a source of entertainment. If you are like me, you would know that this is true. Forget prime time television! There is hardly anything as entertaining as browsing the racks and putting things in your cart.

When you finally get to the checkout counter, it is sort of like an anti-climax but when you fill up your car with hordes of shopping bags, you can't help but feel a little accomplished. Like you have done something.

 An average shopping trip can last about two hours. About the size of a movie so it is a great way to kill time and enjoy yourself.
Only not! Because this "killing" of time also

"kills" your finances and fills up your home with random items that you simply don't need.

→ Loneliness

Boredom and loneliness are intertwined since I mostly do the most damage when I shop alone. Unless I have an equally shopaholic friend tagging along. Though even then, the fear of judgment on someone else's part usually stops me from hoarding unnecessary junk.

At some deep down level, we all are searching for meaningful and worthwhile connections. Especially in today's materialistic world. So when we step out, interact with other shoppers, the store clerks and just get to be around other people, it establishes a sense of false connection. To our minds, it is better than sitting at the couch and snacking on cola and chips.

→ Avoidance

Our current society is built upon the phenomenon of escapism. We want to escape the drudgery of mundane daily life. Watching a man in a cape save a city from burning is far more exciting than typing away at our desks in our offices. We want to escape our normal, everyday routines.

Shopping, just like movies and television, provides us a chance to do just that. We might be facing a huge turmoil in our regular lives. It might be the cusp of a breakup or the bad day at job or simply the horrible weather. The moment we step inside a shopping mall and browse the racks, we can forget all of that.

At that moment, we are nothing but just customers who are there to get some things that they supposedly need. The task is simple. It provides an alternative and it occupies our mind for a little bit of time. For that little bit of time, we forget our very real problems and become a consumer. Nothing could be more simple. Avoidance at its best.

Avoidance is the reason that I shopped the most when I was sad or angry. It helped calm me down. Some people even call it "retail therapy" but it is a paradoxical term. There is no therapy in shopping. Only avoidance of facts and figures.

→ Low Confidence

The world of marketing preys upon the insecurities of the citizens. No matter what age, gender or race, every person on this planet is insecure about something. Marketing plays on that. It tells you that is you use X serum, you will reclaim the glory of youth. That if you shave with Y shaving cream, women will find you desirable again. What are they doing? They are simply targeting your insecurities and your unconscious wants to make you believe that their product will change your life.

Despite falling for clever marketing again and again, both you and I, know that changing your life and building self esteem requires much more than just a shirt, a watch or a cream but it is much easier to go out and get the product than to work on ourselves from within.

→ Control

"Customer is the king"
This is the slogan by which many businesses live. When you are the customer, you have the most say. You get to decide what is best and what is worst. All power is to you.

When you walk into a store, the clerks (especially in high end retail stores) treat you like a celebrity. They walk you, listen to your needs and interests and help you out like you really matter.

This alone is enough to drive many people to swipe their credit cards and hand out their hard earned cash. Simple because, they lack that kind of control in their daily lives.

Let's be real, in our regular everyday lives, most of us aren't VIPs. We are just regular Joes/Janes who take the tube to work and then take it back home. There is nobody in our personal lives to treat us like a celebrity so we retort to those who do. Even if we know deep down that they are only doing it so that they can get our money. At least it provides us with a momentary sense of importance and control.

→ Substitution

It has been noted that many people who have some other kind of addiction (most notably food) give up their former dependency and promote to a shopping addiction. At the surface, it might seem like that the previous problem is gone. There is no longer the problem of binge eating a whole chocolate cake but the thing is that the problem was never the chocolate cake! The problem is likely one of the reasons that I discussed above. What you, or any other person has done is that he/she has substituted the expression of that problem from XX to a shopping addiction.

Can you relate to any of the above symptoms? If yes, then that is what you need to work on to truly conquer your shopping and hoarding problem.

What is a spending ban?

Every addiction is tackled by some sort of therapy and slow withdrawal. Some of you might feel a little apprehensive because I keep referring to the spending habit as an addiction but the fact that this book is in your hands and you're reading it is a testimony in itself that you want to get your spending habits in control because of xyz reasons. I will not linger on those reasons because who can know them better than yourself?

For some of us, it might be so bad that we are in debt, for others it simply accounts for sleepless nights and anxiety because we have not acquired the item that we saw at display today. The intensity can vary but 1 cigarette is also bad and 20 cigarettes are also bad. You should aim to curb both the cases.

So basically, spending ban is a coping mechanism that forces you to keep your spending on check or simply not spend at all.

All shopping addicts have a type. Yes, we are like the bookworms or television geeks. We have a type too. Some shop for food, some shop for clothes and some like yours truly have a tendency to shop for personal care items and home decor. It could be anything but all of us have our specific weaknesses. I know of men who spend thousands of dollars on new fancy gadgets like cameras and phones only to ditch them a few months later when a new model launches.

A spending ban focuses on your area of problem and teaches you to cut off all shopping in that section. Now, a spending ban can be all inclusive or it can allow you a certain "allowance". We'll discuss this later but the main point is that you are not allowed to shop in your specific problem area.

If you have been a shopaholic, which you obviously have been since you have this book, then chances are that you will have plenty of items from your category. So much to last you a lifetime or maybe be enough for a lifetime for ten people. Either way, the main thing is that you don't really "need" any new clothes or gadgets or cans of soda.

That is the main focus of a spending ban. Use. Not Buy.

Your decision to enforce a spending ban could be the result of any number of problems in your life or it could be simply because you want to reclaim your life back from the addiction. Either way is fine as long as you willing to take the initiative.

Many experiences have concluded that simply telling yourself "I need to stop spending so much money" is never really effective. Instead, you should devise out a plan, post it everywhere and keep yourself reminded of it all the time. This is what a spending ban does.

Like other serious addiction recoveries, the recovery from a shopping addiction cannot be gradual. You cannot go from spending a thousand dollars to spending eight hundred dollars and considering that an accomplishment. There is a specific term for addicts like that and it's called "sale shoppers". They blow off horrendous amounts of money on sales and promotions thinking that they "saved" two hundred dollars. No! You didn't save a dime. You burnt what you spent because you didn't need anything you bought.

Hence a spending ban has to be sudden, ultimate and final. The rules are as follows:

→ Figure out your category of problem. Is it food? Home Decor? Candles? Clothes?

Makeup? Gadgets? Watches? Stationary?

Whatever it is, single it down.

→ Do not buy anything from that category. Not even one small equivalent of a pin.

→ You are only allowed to buy necessities like groceries. Some people will overcompensate by buying extra groceries. Hence, only buy things that you can use up within a week or 15 days. No bundle packets of instant coffee are allowed. No matter how good of a deal it is.

→ Set a time limit for your spending ban. Giving it a finite span will keep you motivated. Enforce a spending ban for 30 days, then 60 days and then 90 days and so on.

→ Allow yourself a small present at the end of each successfully finished time span. Doesn't have to be a huge shopping bag filled with clothes. Even a small chocolate would do.

→ Do not seek validation from others. You're doing this for yourself.

→ If someone gives you a present from your problem category, you are allowed to keep and even cherish it.

→ If you want to give someone else a present from your problem category, take someone else along. Someone who will keep you in check. Like a parent, sibling, spouse or a trusted friend. That person's job is to ensure that you don't end up giving presents to yourself as well.

→ Online shopping is completely out of question.

→ Consider it savings for a big goal. Like down payment on a new house or a vacation at some exotic place.

→ Be strict. Be firm.

You can do this!

How to Un-shop?

A shopping addiction is closely associated with a hoarding tendency. The mindset of collecting things and then not using them or at least not using them to their full potential. It is the quintessential problem of "I have nothing to wear" when you actually might have wardrobes full of clothes.

When you shop so much that it becomes an obsessive need, you don't really pay attention to what you have. Instead you become more focused on all that you don't have. For example, I would go out and buy a teal eyeliner even though I had a teal eye shadow that could also be used as a liner. I did that because I was more focused on what I didn't have.

This tendency is the reason that most of us end up accumulating doubles or similar products. You might have several apple scented candles or endless watches or numerous black leggings. In your eyes they are all different but let's be real. Can a lay man differentiate between the two? If the answer is no. Then you have extras.

One of the perks of a spending ban is that you get to explore your already accumulated stash and probably get rid of all the extras and doubles that you might have.

Like me, if you have difficulty letting things go then you might get sweaty palms at the thought of it.

Are you the person who prefers giving money to charity instead of personal belongings?
Do you have some place in your home that is filled with boxes of stuff that you have bought?
Do you save the price tags of clothing that you buy?

Do you keep around broken pieces just because you can't part with them?

If the answer to any of these questions is a grudging yes, then you my friend are in for a treat. It is nothing to fret about because my answer to all these questions is a resounding yes as well. We are both in this together and we both need to learn to "un-shop".

Shopping is an activity where you go out, browse the market, select things, pay for them and bring them home. Un-shopping is the activity where you do exactly the opposite. You rid your home of the excess accumulated stuff. Especially if that is in doubles, broken, junk or never used.

→ Lay it all out

Whatever your problem area is, lay out all the items from that category on a bed or a table or even the floor. If your problem is clothes shopping, then empty all your wardrobes and suitcases. Take out all the clothes and lay them out in front of you.

This might seem unnecessary but trust me it is very useful. You will find stuff that you forgot that you even had. Some of it might even be brand new with tags entact.

Dig deep into the dark corners and retrieve all sorts of things. Go to the dusty attic and take things from there as well. You get the idea. Everything you have, it needs to be in a viewing distance.

→ Sort out

Out of all your items, make four piles.

The first pile should have all the items that you use on a daily or at least weekly basis. Considering the example of clothes again, the first pile should have all the clothes that you repeatedly wear. These include your favorites and your staples like black and white tees, denim and other basic stuff.

The second pile should have all the items that you use at least once a month. Things that might not be your favorite but you still find a way to use them. If I am right, this second pile will be the highest.

The third pile should constitute the items that are occasional, seasonal or reserved for special occasions. Like the fancy crockery that you take out only for Christmas or Thanksgiving dinners. Or that one special designer scent that you wear only when going out on special dates. This will be a small pile most likely.

The fourth pile is going to be the items that you barely ever use, that are brand new or that you had forgotten all about. Depending on your tendencies, this could be the largest pile of all. This is your trouble pile. This is where the un-shopping starts.

→ Use the unused

For the next week or ten days, your focus should be on the fourth pile. You can of course use stuff from the first pile as well because it contains all your basics but you should make a conscious effort to use things from the fourth pile.

Are there some items that you discovered that you love?
Are there some items that you find yourself reaching out for now?
Are there some items that you can't use no matter how much you try?

This effort will answer these three questions for you.

If there are some unopened items, leave them unopened, we will talk about them later.

→ Sort out again

Now that you have put the fourth excess pile to the test, you need to sort it out again. Single out the pieces that you discovered that you love. These will go in your original first or second pile.

The rest of the items need to go. You just put them to the test and you don't need them in any form or any way. Chances are that you don't even really like them and you are just holding onto them because of your hoarding tendencies.

→ Unopened, unused items

In the second sorting, you would have found some items that would be brand new, seals intact and unopened. Out of these, are there some fresh purchases? If yes, then do you have the receipts? If yes, then you need to go and return them. Most retail stores have a great, no questions asked return policy. Even if you don't have a receipt, some stores will allow you to take back the item for store credit. Look into the policies and return as many items as you can.

If you cannot return them, can you gift them to someone?

I always bought gift and value sets because they seemed like a better deal. If you have any unused, new items, look for people in your life who will find a use for them. Is there a lipstick that doesn't look good on your skin tone but might flatter someone you know? Gift it to them.

Younger siblings, younger cousins, aunts, uncles, friends, parents of friends. Just about anybody. If they will use it more than you do, give it away. You can even ask around to see if someone wants it.

If you are too embarrassed to ask around, then another way you can un-shop is by selling the new stuff that you have. You can also sell some pre-loved items but make sure to state the condition accurately.

Make an account on eBay or Amazon and put your items up for sale. There are some rules that you need to follow so read them beforehand. Also, set the prices fairly depending upon the age and the condition of the product. If you are lucky, you might get a buyer. You will get some money and you will be able to un-shop your stash. It is a win-win situation.

→ Donate

This is perhaps the most obvious one but from a recovering hoarder, I know that it is easier said than done. It is very difficult to part from your items but you have to try. It will be tough but since you never used those items anyway, you won't really miss them.

Research your local charities and select one that feels the closest to your heart. You can give your stuff to women charities, charities catering to homeless people, orphanages, shelter homes and basically any charity that you think will find use for them.

You can also sell your items and donate the money to a charity of your choice. Just make sure that the charity is legit and fair. When I un-shopped my stash the first time, I sold most of my unused items and donated the money to a no-kill animal shelter. I felt more happy than I had ever felt after a shopping spree.

What un-shopping will do is that it will make you understand how much of the stuff that you bought is of no use to you. Instead, it was just taking up space in your house and in your life. It will reinforce the idea that a spending ban is necessary because you don't even use half the things that you buy. Hence, you will be more motivated to keep up with the ban.

How to use up?

Project pan and more

I am about a hundred percent sure that you have many "backups" and "just-in-cases" in your stash. You buy something and you like it so much that you go buy it in every color or even several backups of the same color just in case you run out, it gets lost or it is dirty or unavailable. Though let's be honest, how many times do you actually use the back up? Very few, if you ask me. The five pairs of the same tan leggings you have, you probably regularly use only two of them.

Project pan is a side activity associated with a spending ban. It focuses on using up all the things that you have already accumulated. Whether it be back ups, second purchases or just one item. You will be surprised by how much a good quality thing lasts and that you don't really need ten backups after all.

Since you are on a spending ban and you are forbidden from going out and adding new things to your already vast collection, you are forced to work with what you have. This teaches you to be much more creative. You'd be surprised to learn along the way that most things can be used in more than one way. Just because the packaging doesn't state so, doesn't mean that you can't use a product in thousand different ways. You can use a bronzer as an eye shadow. You can use thick leggings as leg warmers. You can use toothpaste as glass cleaner. The options are unlimited. You just have to explore within the limits of your stash to see them.

In fact, the project pan doesn't have to be associated with a spending ban necessarily but the two go hand in hand magnificently.

→ Select five items that come in jars, bottles, pans or tubes.

→ For a start, these five items should be the items that you actually enjoy using or otherwise the project pan would become a chore.

→ These five items cannot be necessities like toothpaste but luxuries like face cream, lotion and barbeque sauce do count.

→ Your aim is to use up these five things. To "hit pan" (or finish tube or hit tub) on them.

→ There is no time limit. You have to keep using them without cheating until you hit pan.

→ Start by taking photos or measurements of your five selected items.

→ Say one of your item is a body butter. You cannot use any other body butter while you are on the project pan.

→ Take progress photos and measurements after some increments like 10 days or so.

→ Keep on using until you finish those five items.

→ Take a break and then select another
    five items.

There are many advantages of starting a
project pan. For one, you will be so occupied
with using what you have that you won't buy
anything more. Secondly, it gives you
perspective about how much time it takes to
actually use up a product. We buy back ups
thinking that if our item of choice ends, it will
be catastrophic but it is nothing of that sorts
because it takes ages to actually wear out or
finish a product.

If you know how long it takes to finish something up, you'll be much more wary of buying more stuff with the misguided intention of using it all up.

Even if your product is limited edition, it will still probably take you ages to finish it up. Unless it's food and you gobble it down like a hungry cave man, there is very little chance that you will actually finish a cream or wear out a shirt until it is in tatters.

You can extend the project pan to clothes and household items as well. For example, wear a pair of jeans until they can't be worn any longer or light a candle until it is gone. If you are obsessed with electronics and gadgets, then keep on using the same phone until it is fulfilling all your needs without any technical glitches.

The main point is to avoid the fluff and get down to the main purpose of things-use and service. Things are there so that we can use them. So that we can benefit from them. Not so that we can line them and then not use them. Clothes were made to be worn, phones were made to be used, cars were made to be driven. If you are not using them that way, then all your money is going to waste.

Use things till you have gotten your money's worth. Only then, buy a replacement.

What people and places should I avoid?

Anyone on a withdrawal can tell you that certain people and places can be triggers. For example, food related holidays (thanksgiving) for people on a weight watch. Of course, at the end of the day, it all boils down to you and your self control but still it is better to not test that patience and avoid certain people and places in the first place.

→ Sales

I am not sure whether this counts as an event or a place but anywhere there is a sale, you

should run in the opposite direction of that.
On the surface, sales seem like a great deal.
Supposedly you are saving a lot of money but
that is not true at all. Sales practically force
you to buy things that you don't need just
because you think that you are getting a better
deal.

The five pack potato peeler that you bought on
sale? Well good luck using them all up until
they wear out

→ Promotional Events

Again both an event and a place. These are those events that brands host to introduce a product. Sometimes they will give away free samples, other times there will be only speeches and marketing promises. Either way, the main aim is to lure you in so that you will hit the nearest store and buy their product.

Don't fall for this.

The simplest way to not fall for this is to not attend at all. In this case, the lesser you know, the better it will be for you.

→ Dollar tree and other run of the mill cheap stores

I am not trying to imply that such stores are bad. I do not intent to come across as pretentious and prudish. The only reason that you need to avoid such places is because you think that just because it is a dollar or so, it is practically free. Well, it's not. 15 items for a dollar or two each are not free. Don't go there. If you absolutely need something, send someone else. If you can't send someone else, make your trip as short as possible and do not browse around.

→ Checkout Counter

This might seem weird but hear me out. Most stores have small items stacked near the checkout counter so that you can pick them up and get them billed as you are leaving. These items are dangerous. You might have popped in just to get bread but you may come out with 15 other trinkets as well. It's best to avoid the checkout counter if you can. Ask the store staff to make your bill. Ask a friend, sibling or another family member. Even if you must face the checkout counter, take only minimal money that will only pay for your intended item. This way you can resist the lure.

→ Door to door salesmen

No. Just No.

When you are trying to avoid shopping, you don't really need an invitation to arrive at your doorsteps. Turn them away as nicely and politely as you can.

→ Sales staff

This especially goes for staff in high end retail stores that works for a commission. They have their own motives for selling an item. Do not believe in the silky sweetness of their promises. Whenever a sales assistant approaches you to ask, "If you need any help?", simply say "No. Thank you" and move on. You don't want to engage in a conversation and you surely don't want to hear them tell you about their wonderful product.

→ Fellow shopaholic friends or family members

This doesn't even need any explanation. The cries of "oh come on", "one little thing won't hurt" and "you deserve this" are enough to sway your resolve. Don't go shopping with such a person, no matter how much you love them. You can do other things to spend time together. It doesn't always have to involve adding items to your cart. Suggest some other activities but don't make a trip to the mall with a fellow shopaholic.

→ Product pushing bloggers/vloggers

The rise of social media has allowed some internet celebrities to surface. These might be your favorite bloggers/vloggers or instagrammers. Most of the time, brands pay such personnel to feature their products.

You might feel like you are talking to a trusted friend but in truth, they are not much different from sales staff working off a commission. If a vlogger offers you his/her personal links, discount codes or the website asks for cookies, run in the other direction. They are making a commission off sales so they will push products down your throat.

It is better to just hit that "unfollow" button.

→ Subscription lists

This isn't exactly a place or a physical person but I felt that this fell in this category. Very often stores will ask for your email address or phone number so that they can keep you "informed".

In the first place, avoid giving your email or phone number to any such business. If you have done so in the past, unsubscribe. There is usually a small hidden clause in the emails that will stop them from coming. Click on it and prevent their inflow.

The case of text messages is a little tricky. Go to one of the shops and ask them to delete your number and stop sending promotional texts to your phone. If you can't do that, simply block the incoming source so that your phone doesn't receive the messages that they send.

 Avoiding some of these might feel hard, even a little extreme but at the end of the day, it is for your mental and financial sanity. With some time, you won't even miss any of it.

How to own less but live more?

This is not a philosophical book so I will not ramble on and on about what true living is and how it is unconnected with material things. While all these claims might be true, this is not the point of this book at all.

Life can have different meanings for different people. Some of us might literally live for food while for others the sole purpose of their existence is their children. These two are just an example. I'm sure that there are 101 other reasons and no person lives for just one particular reason. Our trends, priorities and preferences are ever changing.

Now where do material possessions stand in the midst of this?
They do come somewhere. Saying that they don't matter at all would be a complete lie. To most of us, it matters that we look a certain way or that we eat a certain quality of food. All of this is fine but the real question is that where do these material goods stand in our priority list.

The problem with a shopping addiction is not that material goods like clothes or gadgets matter but rather that they begin to matter more than the core necessities of life. For example, when I was at the peak of my addiction, I would rather eat instant ramen for a week than not buy the new sixty dollars scented candle. My priorities were getting messed up. Addiction came first and health came second.

Isn't it the case with all addictions though?

The main lesson to be learnt from a spending ban is that having things is okay, desiring things is okay as well but what is not okay is to make those things the centre of your universe.

There is much more to living than the things you accumulate and we often tend to forget that as we fill cart after cart.

In the first chapter, we talked about all the deep issues that can be the reason behind compulsive shopping. Those problems won't solve themselves just because you bought a new phone. The new phone is just a distraction. The problem will solve when you will shift you priorities and a spending ban does just that. It practically forces you to reevaluate your priorities.

By the time you are finished with your first trial, you'll have realized that accumulating things is not such big of a deal anyway and that there are way more important things that you'd rather have. Like some peace of mind and a wag of tail from your dog!

Conclusion

Thank you for reading this book.

I hope that you found it of help.

When I was struggling with my own addiction, there was very little help that I could find. That was the reason that I decided to write this book. To extend my helping hand to all those other frustrated people out there. I hope that this book was a little therapeutic and helpful in some way.